(attach)
(photo)

D1473278

WOW...I'm a Big Brother!

My name is _____ , and I live in
(name)

_____ on _____ .
(city and state)   (name of street)

I am _____ years old and these are the things I think a BIG BROTHER should do...

_____

_____

_____

My baby brother
baby sister
(circle one)

is named _____

and was born on _____
(date)

at _____ .
(location)

Where was I when

_____
(baby's name)

was born?... I was with _____

at _____.

I think the baby looks just like

(attach photo or draw a picture)

(attach photo)

The first time Mommy let me hold _____
(baby's name)

was _____.

I think the best thing about belonging to my **family** is

_____ .

MY FAMILY

(attach photo)

Some of the special things that I do with my mommy are _____

_____ .

Shop   Movies   Rake   Games   RAH   tools   Cook   Mow

Some of the special things that I do with my daddy are _____

_____ .

My **little** brother/sister
(circle one)

needs to learn to _____

_____ .

It's my job to **teach**

_____
(baby's name)

to _____

My first word was

_____ ,

and

I think
that the BABY'S
first word will be

Mmm
Coo
Dada
Mama
Ga Ga
Bla Bla
Daddy

Ga Ga
Mama
Bla Bla
Dada
Mommy
Grrr

Mommy and Daddy think
I am an awesome Big Brother
and I think that being a
Big Brother is important because

_____ .

I can't wait for _____

(baby's name)

to be _____ years old so we can

_____ !

-Photos-

-etc...